MW01492604

House of the Lord

THE SALT LAKE TEMPLE.

HISTORICAL SKETCH

AND DEDICATORY PRAYER OF THE

SALT LAKE TEMPLE.

Corner stone laid April 6th, 1853, by President Brigham Young assisted by his counselors, Heber C. Kimball, Willard Richards.

Dedicated April 6th 1893 by President Wilford Woodruff assisted by his counselors, George Q. Cannon, Joseph F. Smith.

Such is the history of the Salt Lake Temple, briefly told in a beautiful art window of one of its upper rooms, the two inscriptions flanking a large center-piece devoted to an accurate representation of the splendid structure, over whose spires, and extending out beyond, appears the motto "Holiness to the Lord."

When Zion is filled with Temples—when, instead of four, her borders may include a hundred, perhaps the succinct record we have quoted will be enough to satisfy the inquiring mind. Not so, however, in this great year of grace, 1893. The reader would fain linger over the sacred theme; for at this writing, April 5th, there are in these mountains but three of these holy edifices dedicated unto the Lord and in operation among His people: the Temple at St. George, begun in November, 1871, and dedicated January 1st, 1877; at Logan, begun in 1877, (the ground being dedicated May 18th, and the corner-stones being laid September 17th, President Young having died in the interim) and dedicated May 17th, 1884; and at Manti, begun April 24th, 1877, by the dedication of the ground, the corner-stones being laid April 14th, 1879, and dedicated May 21st, 1888.

The purposes of this narrative require no extended reference to the Temples at Kirtland and Nauvoo, which were completed, nor to the preparations for like structures at Inde-

pendence and Far West. Still, the historical part of the
sketch would not be complete without a reminder of them.
The Temple at Kirtland, Ohio, which "stood upon a hill and
was the most conspicuous object visible for miles," was pro-
jected in 1833, and dedicated March 27th, 1836. Its cost was
between sixty and seventy thouand dollars. It had occupied
only three years in construction, though part of the interior
at the time of the dedication was in an unfinished state. The
corner-stones of the Temple at Nauvoo were laid and dedicated April 6th, 1841. It was reared amid the direst suffering
and hardships of the people, yet its progress was characterized
by their most willing toil. Parting services were held in the all
but completed buiding in February, 1846, and it was privately
dedicated the following April, after the expulsion. The
foundations of a Temple at Far West were laid on the 4th of
July, 1838, and less than a year afterward, before daybreak on
April 26th, 1839, the Apostles met on the Temple grounds
ordained Wilford Woodruff, who is now the President of the
Church, and George A. Smith to the Apostleship. The Temple
site at Independence, which was secured in obedience to a
command of God, was dedicated August 1, 1831, "by the hand
of Joseph Smith, Jr., and others with whom the Lord was well
pleased."

. This much to refresh the minds of the people who have
come up from far and near to attend and take part in the
dedication of this Temple at Salt Lake City, this most
splendid of all similar structures, this prophetically foretold
House of the Lord which should be reared in the tops of the
mountains, and which now, thanks to the devotion, industry
and generosity of the Saints and the preserving care of the
Lord of hosts, rears its towers majestically into heaven's blue
from the chief city of Zion. To it, during the generation of
time that has been consumed in its erection, the eyes of
the Latter-day Saints in every land have been turned with
loving solicitude. It has been the object of their fondest hopes
and desires, the stout anchor of their faith, the incentive to
their most resolute endeavors. In moments of darkness and
adversity the thought of it and its divine purposes served

ever as a buoy to the drooping spirit. When busy and unscrupulous foes sought provocation against the Saints and in their mocking joy vowed the destruction of the elect, still were the latter undismayed, and the work on their beloved Temple went on. When destroying insects with threatened famine in their train came down from the clouds and covered the land as with a blight, the people's scanty rations were parcelled out with additional care, so that those who labored on the building, either in quarry or on walls, might not have to interrupt their work. So it has gone on during forty years —marking their gladness in prosperity, sanctified by their faith in adversity—but ever and always drawing nearer and nearer the occasion on whose threshold we stand today! Does it not typify in its construction the record of the Church whose members have built it—with its foundation broad and deep, with slow yet steady step marching forward and upward to perfection, with pinnacles pushing ever higher, crowned with the image of one who brought tidings of great joy, the everlasting gospel, to preach to them that dwell upon the earth? Does it not in its various stages represent the condition and circumstances of those whose means and toil have builded it? Its history fully told would be in great measure their history; and since they came to these mountains there are but few pages that cannot be read in the enduring stone of its walls. Looking upon it as another mighty link that shall connect them with the ages that are past and the eternities that are to come, what wonder that in the breasts of the Latter-day Saints the sight, the name, the thought even, of the glorious building arouses a flood of indescribable emotions! In view of all that is past can one wonder that they have awaited with glad anticipation the message that now goes forth: "The House of the Lord in the chief city of Zion is complete, and is now to be dedicated to our God; come, ye faithful, and be partakers of the blessings to be given therein!"

Let us glance back forty years, to that 6th of April, 1853, the twenty-third anniversary of the Church, when the corner-

stones of the Temple were laid. Or rather: let us go back six
years further, to that blazing day in July, 1847, when the
weary feet of the pioneers first pressed the soil of the Salt
Lake Valley. In passing note these coincidences. Brigham
Young lay sick of a fever, but he was tenderly transported
down the hillside in Wilford Woodruff's carriage.

Two days later a party essayed to climb the hills to the

PRESIDENT BRIGHAM YOUNG.

northward, and Brigham Young rode a horse to the top of
Ensign Peak, being preceded by Wilford Woodruff on foot.
Two days more elapse, and on the evening of the 28th Brigham Young, walking upon what we now know as the Temple
Block, strikes the ground with his cane, exclaiming, "Here
will be the Temple of our God;" and Wilford Woodruff forth-
with drives a stake into the ground at the spot designated,

which is, indeed, the center of the Temple today. April 6th, 1853, arrives, and Brigham Young, assisted by his Counselors, presides at the laying of the corner-stones; thirty-nine years later Wilford Woodruff lays the capstone of the building, and one year afterwards, assisted by his Counselors, dedicates the building unto the Lord; Surely there has been more than human design in the connection of our venerable President with the work now at its consummation!

Deserving of detailed description as is the scene that was witnessed that lovely April day forty years ago, we are permitted to dwell upon it but lightly as we pass. It is a rare,

THE QUARRY, LITTLE COTTONWOOD CANYON.

sweet story but it has been many times told. "The sun, the sky, the atmosphere, the earth," writes one who was present, "appeared neither too cold nor too hot nor lukewarm; all seemed filled with life; adapted to each soul, to cheer and make happy every individual of the many thousands of aged, middle-aged and youth, who had assembled from the near and remote parts of the inhabited valley." There was music in plenty from the three bands in attendance; there were flags and banners, military companies and guards; Presidency and Patriarchs, Apostles and Seventies, Bishops and Elders, architects and workmen. The procession moved from the Tabernacle (the old building long since removed) eastward across the block, and, passing through lines of guards, halted at the south-east corner of the Temple ground. President

VIEW OF NORTH-EAST CORNER LOOKING WEST.

Young and Counselors, with Patriarch John Smith, laid the corner-stone, the former delivering the oration, and President Heber C. Kimball offering the prayer. The southwest corner-stone was laid by Presiding Bishop Edward Hunter, his Counselors and the presiding authorities of the lesser Priest-

hood; Bishop Hunter delivering the oration and Bishop
Alfred Cordon offering the prayer. The north-west corner-
stone was next put in place by the Presidency of the High
Priests' quorum and the Presidency and High Council of the
Stake. John Young delivered the oration and George B.
Wallace offered the prayer. The Twelve Apostles, the Presidency of the Seventies and the Elders' quorums officiated at
the fourth corner, the north-east; Parley P. Pratt delivered
the oration and Orson Hyde offered the prayer.

The work so well begun that day has gone on with but
few serious interruptions until the present. Circumstances
have conspired at
times to retard it,
and during the earlier
years almost insup-
erable obstacles made
its progress slow.
But when in place
of three or four yoke
of oxen being neces-
sary to the trans-
portation of a sin-
gle stone from the
quarry twenty miles
distant, there came

VIEW OF THE SOUTH-EAST CORNER.

the change of conditions wrought by the railroad, the walls grew
with greater rapidity; and when at length the time came for the
laying of the cap stone, the event so auspiciously celebrated a
year ago, the anxiety of the people to complete the structure
seemed to burst forth like a pent-up flood. Since the 6th of
April, 1892, there has scarcely been a household in all Israel
in which there have not been daily thoughts and prayers con-
cerning the completion of the Temple. The whole people,
from the highest to the lowest, from the oldest to the youngest,
from the richest to the poorest, took the matter earnestly to
heart; and to the faith and energy of a united people the
building stands forth today a finished and time-defying monu-
ment. We may not omit here an allusion to the ceremonies

LAYING THE CAPSTONE OF THE SALT LAKE TEMPLE AT SALT LAKE CITY, APRIL 6, 1892

of April last, when by unanimous vote the assembled thousands
pledged themselves to furnish the means for the completion of
the Temple so that the dedication might take place a year
later. As on the same date thirty-nine years before, the day
was beautiful, and the services were impressive in the highest
degree. They took place in the presence of the largest
assemblage ever gathered in the Territory, the number on the
grounds being estimated at about 40,000, besides many thous-

ands more who crowded
the adjoining streets
and covered every build-
ing in the vicinity. As
before, the Priesthood
in procession moved
out eastward from the
Tabernacle and took
places upon and around
the stand arranged for
them. A copper plate,
inscribed with histori-
cal data, was exhibited
to the multitude; and
this, with v a r i o u s
C h u r c h publications
and photographs, was
laid in with the cap-
stone. President Joseph
F. Smith offered prayer
after which there was
music from the choir.
President W o o d r u ff
then stepped forward

THE ANGEL.

and said: "Attention, all ye house of Israel, and all ye
nations of the earth! We will now lay the topstone of the
Temple of our God, the foundation of which was laid and
dedicated by the Prophet, Seer and Revelator, Brigham
Young." President Woodruff then pressed a button, opening
an electric current to a contrivance connected with the cap-

stone, the latter being thus released and placed in position on the top of the central east tower. The immense concourse of people, led by President Lorenzo Snow, shouted the hosanna in concert: "Hosanna, hosanna, hosanna, to God and the Lamb, Amen, Amen, Amen." This, was done three times, each shout being accompanied by a waving of handkerchiefs, except when the names of God and the Lamb were uttered. Then there was more singing by choir and congregation and by the glee club, remarks by Elder Lyman, music by the band, an anthem by the choir, and the benediction by President George Q. Cannon. Immediately after these ceremonies the work of surmounting the capstone with the figure representing the angel Moroni was proceeded with. Before night the figure had been placed in position, and its drapery, the flag which enveloped it as it was hoisted into place, was removed. The placing of the ornamental spires on the other towers was continued until all were in place, each being provided with electric lights; the tower walls were washed, pointed and received the finishing touches, and gradually the scaffolding was removed, leaving the building completed and with nothing to mar the sight and study of its magnificent beauty.

With the following figures we close our account of the exterior of the building: The whole length, including towers, is 186½ feet, and the width 99. There are six towers, three on the east and three on the west end of the structure. Other measurements may be summarized as follows:

	To end of rock work	To top of spires.
Height of central east tower	210 ft.	222½ ft.
Height of central west tower	204 ft.	219 ft.
Height of side east towers	188 ft.	200 ft.
Height of side west towers	182 ft.	194 ft.
Height of walls	167½ ft.	
Thickness of walls at bottom	9 ft.	
Thickness of walls at top	6 ft.	
Thickness of buttresses	7 ft.	

The whole resting upon a footing wall 16 feet thick and 8 feet deep The building covers an area of 21,850 feet. The figure of the angel Moroni, which surmounts the central east tower, is of gigantic proportions, being twelve feet five and a half inches in height. The idea conveyed by the statue is that of a herald or messenger, in the act of blowing a trumpet, an embodiment of the fact of Moroni bringing the gospel to the earth in this latter-day dispensation. The figure is admirably proportioned and its pose is graceful. It is made of hammered copper, is gilded with pure gold leaf, and surmounting its crown is an immense incandescent lamp of 100 candle power.

THE INTERIOR.

The stability and grandeur of the building as noted from the outside are found to be supplemented on the inside by the qualities of richness and convenience. Nothing that could contribute to its comfort and elegance has been neglected. It amazes by its massive solidity, and charms with its exquisite beauty; by the ingenuity and completeness of its appointments it delights the most practical, and in its perfection of taste and harmony it dazzles the most artistic and refined.

Enter with us its portals, and let us lead you along the broad corridors, and through the stately rooms, following the route that will be taken by probably seventy thousand Saints during the next two weeks.

We approach from the west across the broad esplanade beneath which is the machinery room, containing four engines and dynamos, with a capacity of two thousand electric lights, as well as the pumps, boilers, etc., and the motive power for the two handsome elevators that operate in the central west tower directly in front of us. To our left, a hundred yards distant, is the boiler house, from which a twelve-inch pipe connecting with the building supplies a most perfect hot water system of heating. We learn also that equally complete are the arrangements for ventilation during warm weather; the pressing of an electric button throws open various transoms and starts sixteen fans, each of one-half horse power.

With less interest in these details because of our anxiety to cross the threshold of the building itself, we hasten up the broad flight of stone steps leading to the south-west entrance. The massive doors which open to us are of heavy, solid oak, with beveled plate glass in the transoms and upper panels, and graceful grills in the form of beehives on the lower panels. The hardware here as in the entire building has been made specially to order.

Turning to the right we reach the circular stairway in the south-west corner tower, and follow its winding steps to the basement. This stairway, which is but one of four—each corner tower being similarly supplied gives an excellent idea of the stability of the structure.

Extending from the basement to the very top, the steps, one hundred and seventy-two in number, are of solid granite, cut by hand, built into the massive walls and the gigantic newelpost of solid masonry; the only woodwork is a wainscoting of heavy oak crowned with molding and relieved by a hand rail; the whole giving an impression of the impregnable castles of the middle ages, built to stand, without crack or quiver, for a thousand years.

Moving northeasterly from the foot of this staircase, a large room divided into a series of compartments is passed and we enter the spacious font rooms solemn yet graceful, impressive yet artistic in all its appointments. The floor is entirely tiled in white marble, which material also serves for the base of the woodwork. The latter is handsomely painted and grained in skillful imitation of bird's-eye maple. All this escapes us, however, as we gaze with profound admiration at the font, which, illiptical in form, occupies the center of the room. It is of cast iron; is reached by a short flight of iron steps at either end, and rests upon the backs of twelve life-sized bronzed oxen, which stand within a railed enclosure sunk some three feet below the main floor. A genuine masterpiece of the artificer is this font, viewing it from whatsoever standpoint we may; for it is large without being oppressive and pleases not less with the massiveness of its construction than with the chaste elegance of its design. By the simplest sort of a contrivance it can be filled with water, or, the water being in, it can be emptied—the entire proceeding requiring but sixteen minutes. The perfection of these arrangements suggests a thought as to the ingenuity employed in other plumbing appliances, and we now examine more closely the numerous colossal bathtubs that are located in the continuous apartments. Hot and cold water are of course at easy reach; there are also improved appliances as to the overflow, small basins within the larger tubs, etc. In this connection, too, due attention should be paid the exquisite onyx wash stands, of which the various floors of the building contain fifteen. Each is of rare beauty, and conveys the impression of an immense gem. Equally unique and costly are five drinking fountains in various corridors—variegated onyx being the material employed. The sanitary arrangements throughout are faultless.

· From the font room we pass across a long, high corridor, which connects by a passage with the Annex to the north of the Temple, and enter a large room in the northeast corner of the building. This room, about forty by forty-five feet in size, is comparatively plain in its decorations and furnishings. It is carpeted in green and is supplied with permanent adjustable chairs. Six large chandeliers depend from the high ceiling.

The next room, reached by crossing toward the southeast, is of almost the same size as the one just described. It also is appropriately carpeted and seated, but the decorator's art has here been agreeably displayed, and walls and ceiling are luminous with warm and natural effects in landscape, beasts and birds. Five splendid chandeliers give evidence that by night the picture would be quite as pleasing as by day.

· Emerging toward the west from this rooom we re-enter

the corridor crossed in-leaving the font room, and come upon
the grand staircase; broad, rich and elegant, and done in
solid cherry. By this staircase we mount from the basement
to the first floor, and notice on the right as we ascend a large
oil painting 12x18 feet, representing "Christ preaching to the
Nephites.'

The opposite wall is adorned with two paintings representing the "Crucifixion" and the "Descent from the Cross."

Turning to the left from the upper corridor we enter another,
the south-west, room of the size of the two last described.
Like the others, it is seated and carpeted. It, too, is gorge-
ously frescoed, and in its harmony of coloring and accuracy
of drawing is as enchanting as a dream. Its general adorn-
ment and furnishings are more beautiful than any yet seen on
this most wonderful and entrancing journey of ours, this
advancement being noticed in every particular from the chandeliers down to the smallest detail.

Next we enter a large room in the north-western part of
the building. This is decorated in white and gold throughout, but judicious taste in the selection of the blue and green
carpet, the richly upholstered seats, the curtains and other
furnishings has removed all suggestions of too dazzling bright-
ness. It is a scene of rare loveliness, pure, restful and exalt-
ing. From its vaulted ceiling hang three grand chandeliers,
but numerous incandescent lights will shed their effulgence
from various points in ceiling, cornice and column. Illuminated, it must present a sight of indescribable splendor. An
art treasure on the south wall is a large dark painting by one
of the old masters, "Joseph interpreting the butler's and the
baker's dreams." On either side of it hangs a glowing scene
in the Holy Land, and in the western end of the room is a
mammoth mirror.

The next room, a few steps higher than the one just
described and scarcely separate from it by an archway, occupies
the north-east part of the building. This room is beyond all
comparison the grandest and loveliest in the entire structure.
Its overhead and side decorations are a perfect ecstacy of
delicate and luxurious color, its magnificent ceiling a sight

worth a voyage round the world to see. No tongue can express, no pen depict in language the marvelous work that has here been accomplished. Like an inspiration, it defies man's best endeavors. Occupying semi-circular alcoves to the east, and high enough to give a fine effect, are two choice paintings—one representing the Hill Cumorah, the other Adam-ondi-Ahman. The chandeliers are of themselves works of

PRESIDENT WILFORD WOODRUFF.

the highest art, the floor is richly carpeted, the furniture is among the finest ever produced on the continent. The prevailing color of the walls is a warm brown, and the effect produced by the contrast with the colors of the twenty Grecian columns that adorn the sides is effective in the extreme. All these columns, all the woodwork indeed, furnish evidence of superb skill in hand-carving. Bracket chandeliers from

the columns and abundance of light from reflected and
cleverly arranged lamps cause the hall when illuminated to
take on an appearance of overwhelming loveliness. Two
colossal triple mirrors occupy places in the east end, and
ascending from this point a narrow flight of stairs leads to an
apartment at the etxreme east appropriately furnished and
designed for the use of the President of the Temple.

PRESIDENT GEORGE Q. CANNON.

But we are not yet ready to leave this enchanting part of
the building, and three smaller rooms, leading off to the south
from the main room, attract our attention. The first, to
which we ascend by a few steps is decorated in rose-pink
and gold, its workmanship throughout is costly, the brackets,
column, etc., being hand-carved and the mirror being one of
the largest and purest in the building. An art glass window

of great size and beauty adorns the south wall; it represents
Moroni delivering the plates to Joseph Smith; and the graceful pose of the angel as well as the eager yet timid expectancy
of the youth are presented with wonderful accuracy. The
furniture of this room is mahogany.

Another small room, reached by a short ascent from the
main floor, is a vision of almost supernatural beauty. It is

PRESIDENT JOSEPH F. SMITH.

circular in form and resplendent in blue and gold, with
borders and panels of red silk velvet. It is paved with an
artistically designed native hard-wood mosaic, the blocks
being mostly no more than an inch square, finely polished.
From the dome which furnishes the ceiling, the light streams
through seventeen circular and semi-circular jeweled windows,
taking a thousand hues as, softened and subdued, it reaches

the interior. The large art window to which the south side of this exquisite little room is given, is a work of surpassing loveliness. It represents the moment in the life of Joseph Smith when he, trusting in the words of the Apostle James, sought wisdom of the Lord, and received as an aswer the visitation of two heavenly beings, one of whom, pointing to the other, said, "This is my beloved son; hear him!" The benignant expression of the two divine personages, their compassionate yet noble attitude, the posture of the lad half in adoration and half shrinking in childish fear, are all delineated with consummate and charming fidelity.

The third small room leading by a couple of steps ascent from the main room is done in sage green and gold, with furniture and trimmings to match. It also has an art-window, and a large plate mirror, and is in all respects as handsome and perfect a little spot as taste and skill can make it.

In these three small rooms last described the most sacred ordinances for the living and the dead are performed.

Passing now finally from the main large room previously referred to, we enter the south-east reception room, not a large, but a most charmingly colored apartment. Cornice and carpet are deep and rich in tone, and the contrast with some of the more delicate hues of which we have seen so much is restful and pleasing. Its woodwork is massive and beautiful. Three other rooms, a suite extending westward toward the main corridor and staircase, answer the purpose of additional reception rooms. In one of them will be noticed a handsome mantlepiece of bird's-eye maple, with base and facings of Utah onyx.

Making our way now to the south-east tower, and again essaying the circular stone stairway, we ascend to the second floor of the edifice and enter a large, light, comfortable but plain room, to be used as the library and recorder's room. It is homelike in its appointments, has eight silver chandeliers, and a good old-fashioned home-made carpet upon the floor. Three semi-circular windows to the north, hung with rare silk curtains, give us a nearer glimpse of the splendid ceiling of the large north-east room on the lower floor previously described; and here we find the proverb contradicted: it is proximity, not distance, that lends enchantment to the view.

From the library we enter a long corridor leading to the west, ranging along the sides of which are six rooms elegantly carpeted and furnished for the presidency of the various quorums of the Priesthood. The most striking of these are the rooms of the First Presidency on the right, and of the Twelve Apostles on the left of the corridor In one of the former apartments is the art window representing the Temple and bearing the inscriptions which we have used as a text in the beginning of this article.

Turning to the right in another short corridor we note two other rooms also for the use of quorums in the Priesthood We are now at the north-west corner and again climb the tower stairs, noticing that in this tower every floor is supplied with fire hose conveniently disposed, so that in case the unexpected, we might almost say the impossible, should happen, adequate remedy and protection would be at hand. In the top of the opposite tower beyond the elavator, is a permanent reserve tank with a capacity of seven thousand gallons of water.

Reaching the next landing stage, the third floor, we enter at once the upper or grand assembly room which occupies the whole extent of the building except the towers; being 120 feet long 80 feet wide and 36 feet high, with a seating capacity of about 2,200 persons. The gallery is of graceful sweep; it is railed with bronze and is reached by circular stairways in each of the four corners. Nothing could surpass the beauteous grandeur of this vast hall. The elevated seats for the Priesthood at either end, the choice hand-carved decorations of dais and balcony, the broad auditorium, the artistically panelled ceiling and frescoed friezed, with innumerable permanent lights mingled in the cornice, and five dependent chandeliers —all combine in presenting to the mind a scene that will be equally imposing by day or by night. The seats in the body of the hall are reversible, so that the audience can face the speaker from either stand. The latter are white and gold with red velvet trimmings and seats.

Here the dedicatory services will be held tomorrow and continued on the succeeding days according to the programme published; and from here, when each service is ended, the audience will descend again by the stairway in the

WEST GATE.

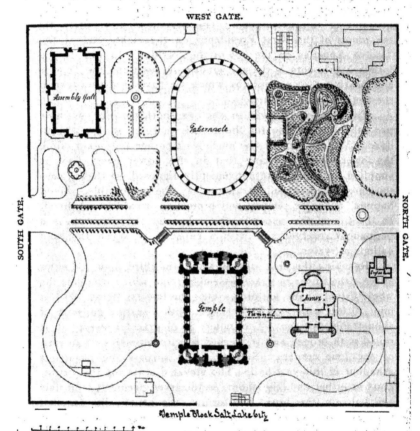

Temple Block Salt Lake City

north-east and north-west towers to the first floor and thence into the open air, the exit from the grounds being by the east and north gates of the block.

We take leave of our readers now, feeling assured that if

they have followed us attentively and have observed the various points of interest in passing, they will agree that from foundation to turret the holy building is wanting neither in solidity, symmetry nor purity. Expense has not been spared, and the Saints we are sure will be glad of it. Their diligence and zeal and liberality have reared and now finished an edifice that in all respects is among the grandest upon the earth, and in at least one respect possesses no counterpart outside of Zion. The completion of a Temple means more to our minds than the mere finishing of a costly pile of masonry. It means that an enduring bond of unity between time and eternity has been welded; it means that the heavens are brought that much nearer the earth; it means that the faith which enables a people to honor God in keeping these His commandments will enable them also to prevail mightily with Him in securing their own salvation and the redemption of mankind. This is a blessed day for Zion and the sons and daughters of Zion in all their abiding places. May its peace and joy and strength abide in their hearts forever!

PRAYER OFFERED AT THE DEDICATION OF THE TEMPLE OF THE LORD.

SALT LAKE CITY, APRIL 6, 1893.

Our Father in heaven, thou who hast created the heavens and the earth, and all things that are therein; thou most glorious One, perfect in mercy, love, and truth, we, thy children, come this day before thee, and in this house which we have built to thy most holy name, humbly plead the atoning blood of thine Only Begotten Son, that our sins may be remembered no more against us forever but that our prayers may ascend unto thee and have free access to thy throne that we may be heard in thy holy habitation. And may it graciously please thee to hearken unto our petitions, answer them according to thine infinite wisdom and love, and grant that the blessings which we seek may be bestowed upon us, even a hundred fold, inasmuch as we seek with purity of heart and fullness of purpose to do thy will and glorify thy name.

We thank thee, O thou Great Eloheim, that thou didst raise up thy servant Joseph Smith, through the loins of Abraham, Isaac and Jacob, and made him a Prophet, Seer, and Revelator, and through the assistance and administrations of angels from heaven, thou didst enable him to bring forth the Book of Mormon—the stick of Joseph, in the hand of Ephraim,—in fulfillment of the prophecies of Isaiah and other prophets, which record has been translated and published in many languages. We also thank thee, our Father in heaven, that thou didst inspire thy servant and give him power on the earth to organize thy Church in this goodly land, in all its fullness, power and glory, with Apostles, Prophets, Pastors, and Teachers, with all the gifts and graces belonging thereto, and all this by the power of the Aaronic and Melchisedek Priesthood, which thou didst bestow upon him by the administration of holy angels, who held that Priesthood in the days of the Savior. We thank thee, our God, that thou didst enable thy servant Joseph to build two Temples in which ordinances were administered for the living and the dead; that he also lived to send the gospel to the nations of the earth and to the islands of the sea, and labored exceedingly until he was martyred for the word of God and the testimony of Jesus Christ.

.   We also thank thee, O our Father in heaven, that thou didst raise up thy servant Brigham Young who held the keys of thy Priesthood on the earth for many years, and who led thy people to these valleys of the mountains, and laid the corner-stone of this great Temple and dedicated it unto thee; and who did direct the building of three other temples in these Rocky Mountains which have been dedicated unto thy holy name, in which Temples many thousands of the living have been blessed and the dead redeemed.

Our Father in heaven, we are also thankful to thee for thy servant John Taylor, who followed in the footsteps of thy servant Brigham, until he laid down his life in exile.

Thou hast called thy servants Wilford Woodruff, George Q. Cannon, and Joseph F. Smith to hold the keys of the Presidency and Priesthood this day, and for these shepherds of thy flock we feel to give thee thanksgiving and praise Thy servant Wilford is bound to acknowledge thy hand, O Father, in the preservation of his life from the hour of his birth to the present day. Nothing but thy power could have preserved him through that which he has passed during the eighty-six years that thou hast granted him life on the earth.

For the raising up of the Twelve Apostles, we also thank thee, our God, and for the perfect union which exists among us   .

We thank thee O Lord, for the perfect organizations of thy Church as they exist at the present time O Lord, we regard with intense and indescribable feelings the completion of this sacred house. Deign to accept this the fourth Temple which thy covenant children have been assisted by thee in erecting in these mountains. In past ages thou didst inspire with thy Holy Spirit thy servants, the prophets, to speak of the time in the latter days when the mountain of the Lord's house should be established in the tops of the mountains, and should be exalted above the hills.

We thank thee that we have had the glorious opportunity of contributing to the fulfillment of these visions of thine ancient seers, and that thou hast condescended to permit us to take part in the great work. And as this portion of thy servants' words has thus so marvelously been brought to pass, we pray thee, with increased faith and renewed hope, that all their words with regard to thy great work in gathering thine Israel and building up thy kingdom on earth in the last days may be as amply fulfilled, and that, O Lord, speedily.

We come before thee with joy and thanksgiving, with spirits jubilant and hearts filled with praise, that thou hast permitted us to see this day for which, during these forty years, we have hoped, and toiled, and prayed, when we can dedicate unto thee this house which we have built to thy most glorious name. One year ago we set the capstone with shouts of Hosanna to God and the Lamb. And today we dedicate the whole unto thee, with all that pertains unto it, that it may be holy in thy sight; that it may be a house of prayer, a house of praise and of worship; that thy glory may rest upon it; that thy holy presence may be continually in it; that it may be the abode of thy well-beloved Son, our Savior; that the angels who stand before thy face may be the hallowed messengers who shall visit it, bearing to us thy wishes and thy will, that it may be sanctified and consecrated in all its parts holy unto thee, the God of Israel, the Almighty Ruler of mankind. And we pray thee that all people who may enter upon the threshold of this, thine house, may feel thy power and be constrained to acknowledge that thou hast sanctified it, that it is thy house, place of thy holiness.

We pray thee, Heavenly Father, to accept this building in all its parts from foundation to capstone, with the statue that is on the latter placed, and all the finials and other ornaments that adorn its exterior. We pray thee to bless, that they decay not, all the walls, partitions, floors, ceilings, roofs and bridging, the elevators, stairways, railings and steps, the frames, doors, windows, and other openings, all things connected with the lighting, heating, and sanitary apparatus, the boilers, engines, and dynamos, the connecting pipes and wires, the lamps and burners, and all utensils, furniture and articles used in or connected with the holy ordinances administered in this house, the veils and the altars, the baptismal font and the oxen on which it rests, and all that pertains thereto, the baths, washstands and basins. Also the safes and vaults in which the records are preserved, with the records themselves, and all books, documents, and papers appertaining to the office of the recorder, likewise the library, with all the books, maps, instruments, etc., that may belong thereto. We also present before thee, for thine acceptance. all the additions and buildings not forming a part of the main edifice, but being appendages thereto; and we pray thee to bless all the furniture, seats, cushions, curtains, hangings, locks, and fastenings, and multitudinous other appliances and appurtenances found in and belonging to this Temple and its annexes, with all the work of ornamentation thereon, the painting and plastering, the gilding and bronzing, the fine work in wood and metal of every kind, the embroidery and needlework, the pictures and statuary, the carved work and canopies. Also the materials of which the buildings and their contents are made or composed—the rock; lime, mortar and plaster, the timbers and lath, the wood of various trees, the gold and silver, the brass and iron, and all other metals, the silk, wool, and cotton, the skins and furs, the glass, china, and precious stones, all these and all else herein we humbly present for thine acceptance and sanctifying blessing.

Our Father in heaven, we present before thee the altars which we have prepared. for thy servants and handmaidens to receive their sealing blessings We dedicate them in the name of the Lord Jesus Christ, unto thy most holy name, and we ask thee to sanctify these altars, that those who come unto them may feel the power of the Holy Ghost resting upon

them, and realize the sacredness of the covenants they enter
into. And we pray that our covenants and contracts which
we make with thee and with each other may be directed by
the Holy Spirit be sacredly kept by us and accepted by thee
and that all the blessings pronounced may be realized by all
thy Saints who come to these altars in the morning of the
resurrection of the just.

O Lord, we pray thee to bless and sanctify the whole of
this block or piece of ground on which these buildings stand,
with the surrounding walls and fences, the walks, paths, and
ornamental beds; also the trees, plants, flowers and shrubbery
that grow in its soil; may they bloom and blossom and
become exceedingly beautiful and fragrant; and may thy
Spirit dwell in the midst thereof, that this plot of ground
may be a place of rest and peace, for holy meditation and
inspired thought.

Preserve these buildings, we beseech thee, from injury or
destruction by flood or fire; from the rage of the elements, the
shafts of the vivid lightning, the overwhelming blasts of the
hurricane, the flames of consuming fire, and the upheavals of
the earthquake, O Lord, protect them.

Bless, we pray thee, Heavenly Father, all who may be
workers in this house. Remember continually thy servant
who shall be appointed to preside within its walls, endow
him richly with the wisdom of the Holy Ones, with the spirit
of his calling, with the power of his Priesthood, and with the
gift of discernment. Bless, according to their calling, his as-
sistants and all who are associated with him in the performance
of the ordinances,—baptisms, confirmations, washings, anoint-
ings, sealings, endowments, and ordinations which are performed
herein, that all that is done may be holy and acceptable unto thee,
thou God of our salvation. Bless the recorders and copyists,
that the records of the Temple may be kept perfect, and without
omissions and errors, and that they may also be accepted of
thee. Bless, in their several positions, the engineers, watch-
men, guards, and all others who have duties to perform in
connection with the house, that they may perform them unto
thee with an eye single to thy glory.

Remember also in thy mercy all those who have labored
in the erection of this house, or who have, in any way
by their means or influence aided in its completion; may they
in no wise lose their reward.
O thou God of our fathers, Abraham, Isaac, and Jacob,
whose God thou delightest to be called, we thank thee with
all the fervor of overflowing gratitude that thou hast revealed
the powers by which the hearts of the children are being
turned to their fathers and the hearts of the fathers to the
children, that the sons of men, in all their generations can
be made partakers of the glories and joys of the kindgom of
heaven. Confirm upon us the spirit of Elijah, we pray thee,
that we may thus redeem our dead and also connect ourselves
with our fathers who have passed behind the veil, and furthermore seal up our dead to come forth in the first resurrection,.
that we who dwell on the earth may be bound to those who
dwell in heaven. We thank thee for their sake who have
finished their work in mortality, as well as for our own, that
the prison doors have been opened, that deliverance has been
proclaimed to the captive, and the bonds have been loosened
from those who were bound. We praise thee that our fathers
from last to first from now back to the beginning can be
united with us in indissoluble links welded by the Holy
Priesthood and that as one great family united in thee and
cemented by thy power we shall together stand before thee
and by the power of the atoning blood of thy Son be delivered
from all evil be saved and sanctified exalted and glorified.
Wilt thou also permit holy messengers to visit us within these
sacred walls and· make known unto us with regard to the
work we should perform in behalf of our dead. And as thou
hast inclined the hearts of many who have not yet entered
into covenant with thee to search out their progenitors and in
so doing they have traced the ancestry to many of thy Saints,
we pray thee that thou wilt increase this desire in their
bosoms, that they may in this way aid in the accomplishment
of thy work. Bless them, we pray thee, in their labors, that
they may not fall into errors in preparing their genealogies;
and furthermore, we ask thee to open before them new

avenues of information, and place in their hands the records
of the past, that their work may not only be correct but complete also.

O thou Great Father of the spirits of all flesh, graciously
bless and fully qualify those upon whom thou hast placed a
portion of thine authority, and who bear the responsibilities
and powers of the Priesthood which is after the order of thy
Son. Bless them all from first to last, from thy servant who
represents thee in all the world to the latest who has been
ordained to the Deacon's office. Upon each and all confer
the spirit of their calling, with a comprehension of its
duties and a loving zeal to fulfill them. Endow them
with faith, patience and understanding. May their lives be
strong in virtue and adorned with humility; may their minis-
trations be effectual, their prayers be availing, and their
teachings the path of salvation. May they be united by the
Spirit and power of God in all their labors, and in every
thought, word and act, may they glorify thy name and vindi-
cate the wisdom that has made them kings and priests
unto thee.

For thy servants of the First Presidency of the Church
we first of all pray. Reveal, in great clearness, thy mind and
will unto them in all things essential for the welfare of thy
people; give them heavenly wisdom, abounding faith, and the
powers and gifts necessary to enable them to preside accept-
ably unto thee over the officers and members of thy Church.
Remember in love thy servant whom thou hast called to be a
Prophet, Seer, and Revelator to all mankind, whose days
have been many upon the earth; yet lengthen out his span of
mortal life, we pray thee, and grant unto him all the powers
and gifts, in their completeness, of the office thou hast con-
ferred upon him; and in like manner bless his associates in
the Presidency of thy Church.

Confer upon thy servants, the Twelve Apostles, a rich
endowment of thy Spirit. Under their guidance may the
gospel of the kingdom go forth into all the world, to be
preached to all nations, kindreds, tongues, and people, that
the honest in heart in every land may hear the glad tidings

of joy and salvation. Overrule, we pray thee, in the midst of the governments of the earth, that the barriers that now stand in the way of the spread of thy truths may be removed, and liberty of conscience be accorded to all peoples.

Remember in loving kindness thy servants, the Patriarchs. May they he full of blessings for thy people Israel. May they bear with them the seeds of comfort and consolation, of encouragement and blessing. Fill them with the Holy Spirit of promise, and be graciously pleased to fulfill their words of prophecy, that thy name may be extolled by the people of thy Church and their faith in thee and in the promises of thy ministering servants may be increasingly strengthened.

With thy servants of the Twelve, bless their associates, the Seventies; may they be powerful in the preaching of thy word and in bearing it to the four quarters of the earth.

May an ever-widening way be opened before them until they shall have raised the gospel standard in every land and proclaimed its saving truths in every tongue, that all the islands and the continents may rejoice in the testimony of the great work thou art in these latter days performing on the earth.

Bless abundantly, O Lord, the High Priests in all the varied duties and positions to which thou hast called them. As standing ministers of thy word in the multiplying Stakes of Zion wilt thou endow them richly with the spirit of their exalted callings. As Presidents, Counselors, Bishops, members of High Councils, and in every other office which their Priesthood gives them the right to fill, may they be righteous ministers of thy holy law, loving fathers of the people, and as judges in the midst of the Saints may they deal out just and impartial judgment tempered with mercy and love.

So also in their various callings, confer precious gifts of wisdom, faith and knowledge upon thy servants, the Elders, Priests, Teachers, and Deacons, that all may diligently perform their parts in the glorious labors thou hast called thy Priesthood to bear.

Forget not, we beseech thee, thy servants the mission-

aries, who are proclaiming the saving truths, that thou hast
revealed for man's redemption to the millions who are now
overshadowed by deep spiritual darkness   Preserve them from
all evil, deliver them from mob violence, may they want no
good thing, but be greatly blessed, with the gifts and powers
of their ministry.   Remember also their families, that they
may be sustained and comforted by thee and be cherished and
cared for by thy Saints.

We pray thee for the members of thy Holy Church
throughout all the world, that thy people may be so guided
and governed of thee, that all who profess to be and call
themselves Saints may be preserved in the unity of the faith,
in the way of truth, in the bonds of peace, and in holiness of
life.   Strengthen the weak, we pray thee and impart thy
Spirit unto all.

Our Father, may peace abide in all the homes of thy
Saints; may holy angels guard them; may they be encom-
passed by thine arms of love; may prosperity shine upon
them, and may the tempter and the destroyer be removed far
from them.   May the days of thy covenant people be length-
ened out in righteousness, and sickness and disease be rebuked
from their midst.   May the land they inhabit be made fruitful
by thy grace, may its waters be increased and the climate be
tempered to the comfort and need of thy people; may drought
devastating storms, cyclones and hurricanes be kept afar off
and earthquakes never disturb the land which thou hast given
us.   May locusts, caterpillars and other insects not destroy
our gardens and desolate our fields; but may we be a people
blessed of thee in our bodies and spirits, in our homes and
habitations, in our flocks and herds, in ourselves and our
posterity, and in all that thou hast made us stewards over.

Now pray we for the youth of Zion—the children of thy
people; endow them richly, with the spirit of faith and
righteousness and with increasing love for thee and for thy
law.   Prosper all the institutions that thou hast established
in our midst for their well-being.   Give to our Church Schools
an ever-increasing power for good.   May the Holy Spirit
dominate the teachings given therein and also control the

hearts and illuminate the minds of the students. Bless marvelously thy servants, the General Superintendent, and all the principals, teachers and other officers, and also those who form the General Board of Education of thy Church. Remember likewise in thy loving kindness the Sunday Schools, with all who, either as teachers or scholars, belong thereto; may the influence of the instruction given therein broaden and deepen, to thy glory and the salvation of thy children, until the perfect day. Bless the members of the General Board of the Deseret Sunday School Union with the wisdom necessary for the proper fulfillment of their duties, and for the accomplishment of the purposes for which this Board was created.

We also uphold before thee the Young Mens' and Young Ladies' Mutual Improvement Associations, with all their officers, general and local, and the members. May they be prospered of thee, their membership be enlarged, and the good that they accomplish increase with every succeeding year. For the Primaries and Religion Classes we also seek thy constant blessing and guiding care; may the spirit of instruction be poured out upon the presidents and associate officers and the teachers. May they keep pace with the rest of the educational establishments in thy Church; so that from their earliest years our children may be diligently brought up in the ways of the Lord, and thy name be magnified, in their growth in virtue and intelligence.

Nor would we forget, O Lord, the normal training classes among thy people, whether these classes be connected with the Church Schools, the Improvement Associations, or the Sunday Schools. Grant that these classes may be the means of spreading true education throughout all the borders of the Saints by the creation of a body of teachers who will not only be possessed of rare intelligence but be filled also with the spirit of the gospel, and be powerful in the testimony of thy truth and in implanting a love for thee and for thy works in the hearts of all whom they instruct.

We would hold up before thee, O Lord, the Relief Societies, with all their members; and all those who preside in their midst according to their callings and appointments, general or local. Bless the teachers in their labors of mercy and charity, who, as ministering angels visit the homes of the sick and the needy, bearing succor, consolation and comfort to the unfortunate and sorrowful. And bless, we beseech thee, most merciful Father, the poor of thy people, that the cry of want and suffering may not ascend unto thee from the midst of thy Saints whom thou hast blessed so abundantly with the comforts of this world. Open up new avenues by which the needy can obtain a livelihood by honest industry, and also incline the hearts of those blessed more abundantly, to give generously of their substance to their, in this respect, less favored brethren and sisters that thou mayest not have reason to chide us for the neglect of even the least among thy covenant children.

O God of Israel, turn thy face, we pray thee in loving kindness toward thy stricken people of the House of Judah. Oh, deliver them from those that oppress them. Heal up their wounds, comfort their hearts, strengthen their feet, and give them ministers after thine own heart who shall lead them, as of old, in thy way. May the days of their tribulation soon cease, and they be planted by thee in the valleys and plains of their ancient home; and may Jerusalem rejoice and Judea be glad for the multitude of her sons and daughters, for the sweet voices of children in her streets, and the rich outpouring of thy saving mercies upon them. May Israel no more bow the head, nor bend the neck to the oppressor, but may his feet be made strong on the everlasting hills, never more, by violence, to be banished therefrom, and the praise and the glory shall be thine.

Remember in like pity the dwindling remnants of the House of Israel descendants of thy servant Lehi. Restore them, we pray thee, to thine ancient favor; fulfill in their completeness the promises given to their fathers, and make them a white and a delightsome race, a loved and holy people as in former days. May the time also be nigh at hand when thou wilt gather the dispersed of Israel from the islands of the sea and from every land in which thou hast scattered them, and the ten tribes of Jacob from their hiding place in the north, and restore them to communion and fellowship with their kinsmen of the seed of Abraham.

We thank thee, O God of Israel, that thou didst raise up patriotic men to lay the foundation of this great American government. Thou didst inspire them to frame a good constitution and laws which guarantee to all of the inhabitants of the land equal rights and privileges to worship thee according to the dictates of their own conscience. Bless the officers, both judicial and executive. Confer abundant favors upon the President, his Cabinet, and Congress. Enlightened and guided by thy Spirit may they maintain and uphold the

glorious principles of human liberty. Our hearts are filled
with gratitude to thee, our Father in heaven, for thy kindness
unto us in softening the hearts of our fellow citizens, the
people of this nation, towards us. That which thou hast done
has been marvelous in our eyes. We thank thee that thou
didst move upon the heart of the President of our nation to
issue a general amnesty. Thou hast removed prejudice and
misunderstanding from the minds of many of the people con-
cerning us and our purposes, and they are disposed to treat
us as fellow citizens, and not as enemies. In this holy house
we feel to give thee glory therefor, and we humbly ask thee to
increase this feeling in their hearts. Enable them to see us
in our true light. Show unto them that we are their friends,
that we love liberty, that we will join with them in upholding
the rights of the people, the Constitution and laws of our
country; and give unto us and our children an increased dis-
position to always be loyal and to do everything in our power
to maintain Constitutional rights and the freedom of all within
the confines of this great Republic.

Remember in mercy, O Lord, the kings, the princes, the
nobles, the rulers, and the governors, and the great ones of
the earth, and likewise all the poor, the afflicted and the
oppressed, and indeed, all people that their hearts may be
softened when thy servants go forth to bear testimony of thy
name, that their prejudices may give way before the truth,
and thy people find favor in their eyes. So control the affairs
of the nations of the earth, that the way may be prepared for
the ushering in of a reign of righteousness and truth. We
desire to see liberty spread throughout the earth to see oppres-
sion cease, the yoke of the tyrant broken, and every despotic
form of government overthrown by which thy children are
degraded and crushed, and prevented from enjoying their
share of the blessings of the earth, which thou hast created
for their habitation.

O God, the Eternal Father, thou knowest all things.
Thou seest the course thy people have been led to take in
political matters. They have in many instances joined the
two great national parties. Campaigns have been entered
upon, elections have been held, and much party feeling has
been engendered. Many things have been said and done
which have wounded the feelings of the humble and the meek,
and which have been a cause of offense. We beseech thee,
in thine infinite mercy and goodness, to forgive thy people
wherein they have sinned in this direction. Show them, O
Father, their faults and their errors, that they may see the

same in the light of thy Holy Spirit, and repent truly, and sincerely, and cultivate that spirit of affection and love which thou art desirous that all the children of men should entertain one for another; and which thy Saints, above all others, should cherish. Enable thy people hereafter to avoid bitterness and strife; and to refrain from words and acts in political discussions that shall create feeling and grieve thy Holy Spirit.

Heavenly Father, when thy people shall not have the opportunity of entering this holy house to offer their supplications unto thee, and they are oppressed and in trouble, surrounded by difficulties or assailed by temptation, and shall turn their faces towards this thy holy house and ask thee for deliverance, for help, for thy power to be extended in their behalf, we beseech thee to look down from thy holy habitation in mercy and tender compassion upon them, and listen to their cries. Or when the children of thy people, in years to come, shall be separated, through any cause, from this place, and their hearts shall turn in remembrance of thy promises to this holy Temple, and they shall cry unto thee from the depths of their affliction and sorrow to extend relief and deliverance to them, we humbly entreat thee to turn thine ear in mercy to them; hearken to their cries, and grant unto them the blessings for which they ask.

Almighty Father, increase within us the powers of that faith delivered to and possessed by the Saints. Strengthen us by the memories of the glorious deliverances of the past, by the remembrance of the sacred covenants that thou hast made with us, so that, when evil overshadows us, when trouble encompasses us, when we pass through the valley of humiliation, we may not falter, may not doubt, but in the strength of thy holy name may accomplish all thy righteous purposes with regard to us, fill the measure of our creation, and triumph gloriously, by thy grace, over every besetting sin, be redeemed from every evil, and be numbered in the kingdom of heaven amongst those who shall dwell in thy presence forever.

And now, our Father, we bless thee, we praise thee, we glorify thee, we worship thee, day by day we magnify thee and give thee thanks for thy great goodness towards us, thy children, and we pray thee in the name of thy Son, Jesus Christ, our Savior, to hear these our humble petitions, and answer us from heaven, thy holy dwelling place, where thou sittest enthroned in glory, might, majesty and dominion, and with an infinitude of power which we, thy mortal creatures, cannot imagine, much less comprehend. Amen and amen.

STANDARD CHURCH WORKS.

Book of Mormon, Large Print,

Full Cloth	$1.75
Full Leather	2.25
Full Leather, Gilt	3.00
Full Morocco, Gilt	3.75

Book of Mormon, Small Print,

Cloth	1.00
Roan	1.25
English Roan	1.75
Calf Grain, Gilt	2.50
Morocco, Extra Gilt	3.00

Doctrine and Covenants, Large Print,

Full Cloth	1.75
Full Leather	2.25
Full Leather, Gilt	3.00
Full Morocco, Gilt	3.75

Doctrine and Covenants, Small Print,

Cloth	1.00
Roan	1.25
English Roan	1.75
Calf Grain, Gilt	2.50
Morocco, Extra Gilt	3.00

Hymn Book, 2nd edition,

Cloth	.35
Roan	.75
Calf Grain, Gilt	1.00
Morocco, Extra Gilt	1.50

Voice of Warning,

Cloth, limp covers	$ .25
Cloth, stiff covers	.35
Leather	.50
Calf Grain, Gilt	1.25
Morocco, Extra Gilt	1.50

Key to Theology,

Cloth	.75
Roan	1.00
Calf Grain, Gilt	1.60
Morocco, Extra Gilt	2.00

Spencer's Letters,

Cloth	.75
Roan	1.00
Calf Grain Gilt	1.60
Morocco, Gilt	2.00

Pearl of Great Price,

Cloth	.50
Cloth, Gilt	.60
Leather	.75
Leather, Gilt	1.00

A Compendium of the Doctrines of the Gospel, by Franklin D. Richards and James A. Little,

Cloth	1.00
Leather	1.25
Morocco, Extra Gilt	1.75
Morocco, Gilt, with tuck	2.00

Ready References, at 45, 55 and 85 cents, and with tuck at $1.10 each, net.

FAITH ○ PROMOTING ○ SERIES.

My First Mission,	- -	$ .25
A String of Pearls,	- -	.25
Leaves From My Journal,	-	.25
President Heber C. Kimball's Journal,	- - -	.25
Early Scenes in Church History,	- - - -	.25
Fragments of Experience,	-	.25
The Life of Nephi,	- -	.25
Scraps of Biography,	-	.25
The Myth of the Manuscript Found,	- - - -	.25
Labors in the Vineyard,	-	.25
Eventful Narratives	- -	.25

Geo. Q. Cannon & Sons Co.,

P. O. Box 460.   SALT LAKE CITY.

CPSIA information can be obtained
at www.ICGtesting.com
Printed in the USA
LVOW02*0252270417

532373LV00003B/52/P

9 781362 664109